Coyotes Always Howl at Midnight

Tales of a '70s Rancher's Wife

Audrey Keen-Hansen

Order this book online at www.trafford.com/06-2506
or email orders@trafford.com

Most Trafford titles are also available at major online book retailers.

Note for Librarians: A cataloguing record for this book is available from Library
and Archives Canada at www.collectionscanada.ca/amicus/index-e.html

Printed in Victoria, BC, Canada.

ISBN: 978-1-4251-0748-2

*We at Trafford believe that it is the responsibility of us all, as both individuals
and corporations, to make choices that are environmentally and socially sound.
You, in turn, are supporting this responsible conduct each time you purchase a
Trafford book, or make use of our publishing services. To find out how you are
helping, please visit www.trafford.com/responsiblepublishing.html*

*Our mission is to efficiently provide the world's finest, most comprehensive
book publishing service, enabling every author to experience success.
To find out how to publish your book, your way, and have it available
worldwide, visit us online at www.trafford.com/10510*

www.trafford.com

North America & international
toll-free: 1 888 232 4444 (USA & Canada)
phone: 250 383 6864 ♦ fax: 250 383 6804
email: info@trafford.com

The United Kingdom & Europe
phone: +44 (0)1865 722 113 ♦ local rate: 0845 230 9601
facsimile: +44 (0)1865 722 868 ♦ email: info.uk@trafford.com

10 9 8 7 6 5 4

If one advances confidently in the direction of her dreams,
and endeavors to lead a life that she has imagined,
she will meet with success unexpected in common hours.

(With apologies to Henry David Thoreau)

For the children — Chris, Ann, and Mark — who shared the adventure.

Contents

INTRODUCTION

ONE DAY, in a contemplative mood, I realized that a piece of my life was becoming lost in the quick step of near–term experiences.

Was it odd, I wondered, that a city person like me had joined the exodus to Colorado in the early 1970s – a time of hippies, John Denver's songs, and "Colorado High" – and had experienced a Western life previously only conceived of in fantasy?

Did it matter, I wondered, that I'd been widowed young and raised my son – from his ninth month through thirteenth year – alone, all the time pursuing a career, desperate to provide him a good life, pushing back loneliness that I had not had time to alleviate?

I was 42-years-old, a veteran of the equal rights movement. I'd taught at a university and established the school's first women's program. I was independent. Yet I had thrown that life to the wind to become a rancher's wife, a stepmother, and had entered a brand-new world in the West.

I decided to save the memories. I wrote down those that caused so much happiness and satisfaction, so much anguish and frustration.

Western literature is full of old-time sheriffs, wagon train diaries, cowboys and Indians. Could there be room for a woman's latter-day experiences full of trial, error, and adventure?

I wonder.

COYOTES ALWAYS HOWL AT MIDNIGHT
Tales of a Rancher's Wife

PROLOGUE

SILENCE BLANKETED our valley on summer mornings, broken only by a meadowlark's song or the crow of a distant rooster. Over at the crest of the mountains, bright lemon sunshine crept into a wide and empty sky.

We arose early one such morning, my husband Veryl and I, determined to manicure our long–neglected lawn. A twenty–foot band of green bordered three sides of our sprawling adobe ranch house.

As usual, Veryl mowed. I, assigned to the electric edger, whacked at misfit blades of grass that sprouted haphazardly along the house wall. *A mindless task*, I always thought.

This morning as I jabbed at the growth with my usual abandon, my thoughts easily drifted elsewhere. Like the good little rancher's wife I felt I should be, I mentally listed errands we had to run in town later in the day.

Don't forget the feed store for dog food, I reminded me. (We always bought the 50-pound sacks for our three Australian Shepherds: Happy, Dusty and Augie.)

Wonder if I'll have time to stop at Kavely's, the town's one-story department store with its merchandise stacked on tables in neat piles. *Will Sear's have our order in?*

I'd almost finished the first side of the house when suddenly the edger balked. The unexpected jerk almost pulled the lightly held machine from my grasp. Abruptly, my thoughts snapped back to the job at hand.

I bounced the machine up and down on the grass a few times. The engine whirred. No grass fell. Puzzled, I pushed down, harder. Same response. Finally, overwhelmed by curiosity, I lifted the edger to take a look.

My shriek must have been heard from Colorado to the Mexican border.

In front of me dangled a two-foot-long *snake* – its head caught in the edger.

Veryl, already at work on the other side of the house, yelled, "What happened?" He kept on shouting as he sprinted around the corner.

I saw him, but I couldn't speak. Instead, I swung the edger in his direction – and *gestured* a lot.

Unexpectedly, his pace slowed. His initial expression of concern turned into a whimsical grin, then he nonchalantly sauntered in my direction. Without a word, he detached the machine from my clenched hand, and began eyeing the snake up and down like a doctor assessing a patient – *complete with a frown, pursed lips, and his head shaking in feigned regret.*

"Mmm," he muttered at length. "You sure did a good job on him."

In shock, I watched him remove the snake with his bare hands, then throw it into the chicken pen.

Now *he* may have assumed, "Well, that's the end of that," but *I* pictured chickens pecking at that grisly horror. I saw myself finding it suddenly underfoot when I fed our flock.

"Get that thing out of there!" It sounded like another scream.

Dutifully, Veryl went in, picked up the snake, and flung it out into the pasture.

I assumed he knew my grass-edging days were over.

TALE ONE

Colorado, Here I Come!

1
The Little Kingdom

THE NAME of our ranch, "Poco Reino," was burned into a wood slab that hung high between two poles at the entrance. Though not good Spanish, "Poco Reino" intended to describe the place as a "little kingdom."

And indeed the ranch wasn't big. Just a 55-acre piece of Colorado's San Luis Valley, three miles east of Alamosa, divided into a few somewhat scrubby alfalfa fields, several pastures, a boggy pond fed by ground water, a chicken pen that at one time held 65 chickens, a vegetable garden, and the five acres where our eight-room adobe house stood.

I had arrived at Poco Reino – along with my blond, blue-eyed son Chris, age 13 – after marrying the man who owned it, a man whom I thought embodied the look of all those rugged cowboys I'd read about and seen on the movie screens. He was tall, lanky, and had a slow deep Oklahoma drawl. In jeans and boots, he fit my image of a Western rancher perfectly.

Both of us had been widowed and left with young children. (His were Mark, age six, and Ann, age eight.) Put the families together, we thought, and *voila'* the kids have a mother and father; mother and father have companionship and help in raising these "young-uns."

Also *I* would have, I assumed, the expected high adventure that drew me to this part of the world.

Being a rancher's wife had been among my dreams (largely due, I later determined, to John Denver's songs about Colorado). But, in reality, the ranch was Veryl's hobby; he spent his days as a biology professor at nearby Adams State College.

I had never lived on a farm, a ranch, or "in the country" before. Nor had I interacted with any animal, other than a dog. Circumstances, however, soon provided me with more comprehensive experience, and I surprised myself when I realized early on that I held genuine affection for life in this remote high desert area. It grew on me slowly, subtly.

Almost every morning, after Veryl left for the college and the children had safely boarded the school bus, I stood, exhilarated, looking at the valley from north to south and east to west.

The San Luis Valley is sizable – about 80 miles wide and 100 miles long. Some say it's larger than Rhode Island, Connecticut, and Delaware combined.

Three sides are dominated by the high bulk of the San Juan and Sangre de Cristo Mountains; many of these designated Colorado "Fourteeners," or more than 14,000 feet above sea level. Snow often remains on these jagged peaks ten months out of twelve. The scene can cause gasps of wonder. Huddling against the eastern mountains, too, are some of the highest sand dunes in North America.

South range the "Brownie Hills," irregular rocky mounds of lava forged in a distant turbulent past. Beyond these, the valley widens and blends into New Mexico, about 35 miles from our ranch.

The Rio Grande River, not yet tamed by dams and flowing free, streaks across the flat valley floor from its birthplace in the San Juans, and turns south at Alamosa on its long journey to the sea.

The land itself, however — except for some farms, a few small towns, and widely dispersed ranches — is a desolate expanse of chico bushes, rabbit brush, assorted cacti, and alkaline-pieced adobe sand — all hiding a mix of insects, rabbits, lizards, coyotes, snakes, and who-knows-what.

Eventually I got used to it all . . . except maybe the snakes!

2
The Young Ranch Hands

WHEN I BEGAN this challenging experience in the "outback" of Colorado, I was not unaware of the formidable task involved in step-parenting two small children whose mother had died two years earlier, and integrating a son who, when he was less than a year old, had lost his father in death as well.

(Veryl's only true offspring was Ann; husky, redheaded Mark had been adopted as a baby.)

Veryl and I had assumed, I guess, it would all work out. Not a lot of discussion beforehand about how the melding of two families would take place, just confidence in our own intelligence and abilities. We tried to create an atmosphere wherein it was taken for granted that all were "our" children.

Ann and Mark were young, and I think I had the easiest job there.

Slim and strong like her father, Ann was a quiet girl. A latent streak of temper occasionally surfaced, however, and fights between her and Mark became common. In the actual physical struggles I observed, the winner was always Ann.

Six-year-old Mark tried very hard to please. Of all the children, he worked the hardest to keep his room neat and did the least complaining. He seemed so physically strong, yet emotionally he needed a lot of love. I'll never forget his tears a few years later when he wondered why his real mother hadn't wanted him – and why his "second" mother had died. I held him tight . . . and I had no answer.

Chris being older, and without ever knowing a father, may never have found the love and acceptance he wanted and needed from Veryl. Yet, although initially out of his element as far as ranch life was concerned, Chris worked hard to be a "Westerner." But I always worried about his happiness.

Big for his age when we arrived at the ranch, Chris helped Veryl build fences and a corral, assisted in breaking horses, and took on other ranch-type chores. Before long he was developing muscles, many the result of lifting heavy hay and alfalfa bales while feeding the cattle and horses.

One of these muscle-building experiences was about to occur the late afternoon I received an urgent phone call from Veryl. He had driven with Chris to a farm near La Jara, about twenty miles south, to pick up a truck load of alfalfa. (Our acres usually didn't produce enough of this crop to feed all our animals.)

"We've had a flat tire down here," Veryl said, "and from the look of things, we're not going to make it back for dinner." The clock showed four in the afternoon.

"Why so late?" I said. "Anything I can do?"

"Well, the problem is the bales are already on the truck. We'll have to unload them all to change the tire . . . and then reload." I heard him sigh. "It's going to take a while. Any chance you can bring down some food?"

"No problem. I'll put something together right now, " I said, surprised and concerned. "Tell me how I can find you."

After getting the directions, I told him he could expect me in about three-quarters of an hour.

I made a generous quantity of sandwiches, filled a thermos with coffee, grabbed a six-pack of soda, and took off.

When I found them, Chris and Veryl had just finished unloading the heavy rectangular bales that had been piled high and had towered above the truck bed. Both looked exhausted.

They stopped to eat, then tackled the flat tire as the dark of night approached. Finally, the reloading began.

I attempted to help, but my meager strength was no match for the weight of a bale. So, I just waited and inwardly felt the pain of these two men while they grunted and heaved the alfalfa back onto the truck.

When they were finished, I drove behind them back to the ranch, silently admiring both, but admittedly full of a mother's pride for her young city-bred son.

3
Changes

PREVIOUS YEARS in the city became a blur as I settled into this new ranch life.

My wardrobe had changed abruptly. I had arrived at Poco

Reino with just one pair of flat shoes – brown penny loafers; the rest were heels that matched an office life.

Within days, however, I owned a pair of high-top western boots, and Veryl had insisted that I add a pair of hiking boots as well for our planned excursions into the mountains.

Daily garb became blue jeans and flannel shirts, and I kept handy a heavy winter jacket – an item needed year-round for our trips to the high country where weather changes fast.

I discovered shortly that Alamosa – even though its population of 8,000 made it the largest town in the valley – provided limited shopping opportunities, and I surprisingly found myself eagerly anticipating the arrival of each new Sears, Penney's, and Wards catalogue. In time, we ordered everything from clothing to chicken feeders and fencing from these.

For larger purchases, such as furniture or a car or truck, we drove either east over 9,500–foot–high La Veta Pass to Pueblo, Colorado, a distance of 125 miles, or to Santa Fe, New Mexico, about 150 miles south.

Revelation followed revelation.

For instance, I learned that the anonymity common to a big city – where people ignore most passing humanity – did not prevail in the valley. Here, everyone required recognition, even those I didn't know.

Veryl, surprised and chagrined by my lack of proper rural etiquette, instructed me as follows:

  ✦   When you drive down a country road, raise your hand from the steering wheel and wave to everyone coming your way, whether in a vehicle or on foot.

  ✦   When you walk down Main Street, look into the window of all passing cars and wave – even if you only *think* you know the person inside.

*   In fact, when walking anywhere, you must raise your hand, smile, and say "Hi!" to everyone you meet.

I became the best little "hand-raising-est" woman in the valley.

4
Sure, I Had a Honeymoon

THREE WEEKS after I arrived at the ranch, we bought a navy blue Dodge station wagon – after all, our new family of five needed to be accommodated. Shortly thereafter, Veryl suggested we take a trip to Mexico City, a kind of honeymoon. We would leave Ann and Mark with their grandparents in Houston, Texas, he said, then take Chris with us.

Not that I didn't love my son, but I thought to myself, "Some honeymoon." But that's the way it came to pass.

To get to Houston, we drove through the Oklahoma panhandle and across the entire State of Texas, spending only one night on the road – in Amarillo, where all five of us bedded down in the same motel room.

After dropping off Ann and Mark, we continued down the Texas coast to Brownsville. We made a timely crossing of the border only after Veryl bribed a border guard with twenty dollars to "get on with it."

Thus began our long trip into Mexico. We lacked only one seemingly important talent: none of us spoke Spanish.

Chris had brought about a dozen books with him and spent much of the ride in the back seat, reading. (When we stopped overnight, this thirteen-year-old had a separate room where, he later confided to me, he lay half-awake all night, scared to death.)

Our first real stop was Tampico, a city on Mexico's east coast once famous for a beach described in a song of the 1940s. For some unexplained reason, Veryl wanted to see this beach.

No one we met seemed to understand English, so we made a necessary purchase, an English-Spanish dictionary. After many halting references to this book, we finally found someone who understood, and who could direct us to the beach, *la playa*. We were disappointed to find this attraction deserted, its white sand littered with debris.

This adventure seemed a harbinger of what was to come.

Nevertheless, we drove on. Over the mountains into the crowded traffic-clogged streets of Mexico City, then later back over the mountains (nearly skidding off a narrow, no-shoulder road in the rain) through Monterrey to Houston.

In between we saw cities and a culture new at least to Chris and me — but we missed visiting the historic ruins, arrived at the archaeological museum after closing time, and had a flat tire in some small town, where a little boy said his uncle could fix it (and he did).

But really, this was no "honeymoon" to write home about.

5
The Gun Slinger

EARLY ON, I also learned to shoot a gun. I rebelled at first. I didn't even want to touch it. But Veryl had said: "You're going to be alone out here, you know." (We lived in an open area three miles east of town.) "I hope you'll never have to use it, but this skill could save your life."

I tried to argue. "But, but I . . ."

"You're going to learn to shoot!" And that, I was given to

understand, was the final word.

So one sunny day, Veryl and I walked to the small pond on our back twenty acres for my shooting lesson. We stood on the raised, cattail-covered bank and, with magpies and noisy yellowhead and redwing blackbirds as an audience, Veryl showed me how the gun operated.

Calmly and confidently, he fired at a few rabbit holes, then thrust the pistol into my hands.

"Go ahead. Shoot," he said.

With trepidation, I aimed at a hole, closed my eyes, and pulled the trigger.

"Again. This time with eyes open," he said. I shot.

"Again . . . again . . . again." That's all I seemed to hear. After emptying a second clip, I noticed Veryl frowning and scratching his head.

"Well, if you want to protect yourself someday, I guess we'd better plan on a few more lessons."

Relieved this session was over, I handed back the gun and internally shuddered, dreading the thought of actually aiming this weapon at some beast or human and then pulling the trigger.

As it was, my second lesson was somehow forgotten. The gun went back into its box, was placed on a closet shelf, and remained there.

Fortunately, I never had a reason to use it.

6
Our Adobe Hacienda

I LOVED our sprawling eight-room, all adobe, house. It was only two years old when I moved in, and its southwestern architecture incorporated all that style's delights.

Our large living room had a small rounded fireplace nestled in a corner from which *bancos*, built-in benches, ran off on two sides. *Vigas*, large hand-hewn logs, and *latillas*, slats of wood, made up the ceiling. And from the room's two large windows facing east, we beheld a panoramic view of the Sangre de Cristo mountains, ever-changing with the seasons.

Two of our home's three entrances featured *portals* – a type of porch with an open log top held up by more logs; the third led into the garage.

As in most southwestern homes, our walls were white. The Moorish designs of Mexican wall tile decorated the kitchen and bathrooms. All light fixtures came from Mexico. In the living room, a beautiful red Navajo rug hung on the wall above a large dark-wood Mexican couch.

(Each Easter vacation Veryl attached our small camper to the station wagon, and our entire family drove down to the border town of Juarez, Mexico, to find any authentic decor pieces we might possibly lack.)

Outside, near the road, stood a tall adobe pump house that Veryl had attempted to match to the exterior of the house. He had made the adobe bricks for it himself out of clay and straw, then hired a local craftsman to build it. Its purpose was to shelter a small pump that brought up the ground water used to irrigate our lawn and garden.

To me, however, this building – complete with its small

window in the door – looked like the fanciest outhouse in the neighborhood!

7
Chokecherry Moments

NO DOUBT about it, there's work involved in taking care of a big house, three children, ranch chores and . . . a husband *who comes home for lunch.*

My days definitely needed to be organized. And the first thing I organized was housework.

I determined which jobs Ann, Mark, and Chris could handle, then made up three lists, which I posted. These were rotated weekly, and included such things as cleaning out the dishwasher, setting and clearing the tables, dusting (I hated to dust; so did the kids), and cleaning the bathtubs.

To help in the time-consuming preparation of vegetables from the garden, I invented competitions for Ann and Mark, who snapped the beans and shelled the peas.

I also taught all three how to change and make their own beds, and expected them to do so. All sorts of grumbling, of course, but as time went by, the chores became routine.

My labors included daily mopping of the Spanish-tile floors of the kitchen and the long hallway between the bedrooms, since dust and sand from outside came in with every footfall. Laundry and ironing for five proved no picnic ether.

Most days I also fed the chickens (up to 65 in two pens), gathered eggs, tended two flower beds, watered the fifty trees we had planted at the perimeter of our property, and sewed when necessary.

Often I made jams and jellies, all kinds. (Occasionally, Veryl and I would travel out to the mountains alone and pick chokecherries along the banks of swift-flowing streams for this purpose.) One year I won a blue ribbon at the fair for my strawberry-pineapple jam.

Of course I also baked and cooked — always trying to meet the time line that pretty much ended when the children arrived from school around four.

I really never complained about my life, however — at least not early on. And best of all, I felt such smug satisfaction when I realized that all the children had begun calling me "Mom."

TALE TWO

Critters, Cookpots, and Catastrophes

Not All Food Comes from the Supermarket?

WHEN I MARRIED Veryl, I discovered that cooking for an Oklahoman would indeed be a test of my culinary abilities.

My introduction not only to unfamiliar foods, but also to where such foods came from, began during my first week at the ranch when I answered the telephone.

"Hello?" I said.

An unfamiliar female voice responded. "This is Nelson's Dresses. Your beast is ready."

"What?!?" I said, not comprehending. To say the least.

"This is Nelson's Dresses. The beast you ordered is ready."

"Oh," I said, and not wanting to appear stupid, I thanked the voice and hung up. The caller's words, however, raced around in my head. I flirted with the thought that this had perhaps been an obscene call.

I told my new family about it.

Veryl smiled throughout my tale; then he actually guffawed.

"That was Nelson's Dressed Meats. My *beef* is ready," he laughingly explained. Even Ann and Mark were snickering now. ("Ha, Ha," I thought.)

"I'm sorry," he continued, obviously trying to control himself. "I ordered it before you arrived."

I was chagrined, not quite understanding what he was talking about. But I learned that day that we ordered beef by the side – and I was given to understand a "side" is one-half of a butchered steer – from Nelson's Dressed Meats, a meat processor twenty miles away. We later would use that same firm to butcher our own hogs, sheep, and cattle.

Other foods also came from unexpected places.

At the right time in spring, we would drive out on long empty ranch roads and pause to pick tender, wild asparagus along the way. In fall when potatoes were harvested in Rio Grande County, we drove twenty miles or more to pick up potatoes from the road. They had fallen off trucks headed for storage cellars.

2
Ham Hocks and Beans

MY WISCONSIN upbringing also did not prepare me for whipping up meals containing other foods my husband adored — pinto beans and ham hocks, biscuits and gravy, cornbread, black-eyed peas, okra, collards, mustard greens, fried apples, and molasses cake.

Except for cornbread, I had never eaten any of these, let alone cooked them for a family of five. But I resolved to do my best.

Veryl became my teacher. After first instructing me in what some of these foods looked like, he introduced me to the pressure cooker, which he said would cut preparation time, especially of pinto beans.

I guess he assumed I knew how to operate it, but somehow I had grown up without ever experiencing the joy of using this cooking vessel. Not wishing to appear simple-minded, however, by asking how a pressure cooker works, I instead studied the directions in a cookbook for my first try. It seemed simple enough.

In went beans, ham hocks, some water, some seasoning – as Veryl had instructed me. Soon a little steam vent on top of the cooker was tapping a merry rhythm.

That evening the patience of my hungry family began to wear thin, and I heard grumbling – "We're hungry" – from the living room where all were watching TV.

Well, I thought, the beans have been cooking for some time, they must be done. I unlatched the cover of the cooker to take a look.

Pow! Beans hit the ceiling and me at the same time.

I screamed. Everyone came running, then they had the nerve to laugh. I saw absolutely no humor in my being covered with hot dripping beans, but for some reason, the others did.

I then noticed some beans still in the pot. I wiped myself off as best I could, avoided spaces on the floor still swimming in beans, and finally announced dinner would be served.

I put the ham hocks and beans in a large serving bowl and

brought out the fried okra – also prepared according to my husband's instructions – and freshly-baked cornbread. Eagerly, the family dove into to the meal.

Almost as eagerly, they all put down their forks, and grimaced.

"I assume you washed the beans first," said Veryl, eyebrow raised.

I took a forkful of the beans myself and tasted . . . sand. No one had told me to *wash* the beans.

This turned out to be a bad day all around.

As time passed, though, ham hocks and beans became my specialty.

3
A Vegetable Garden Saves Money

OUR VEGETABLE garden grew next to the chicken pen — a good source of manure — and over the septic tank.

In reality, it was Veryl's garden. He grew asparagus, beans, peas, carrots, lettuce, and other things from year to year.

He experimented, too, with odd offerings from the seed catalog: blue potatoes, purple beans, and giant radishes.

Omitted from this vegetable patch, however, were tomatoes and corn. These required a growing season much longer than that available in our valley, where frost often arrived before the end of August.

Beans, green and yellow, were another touchy vegetable. They froze if the temperature only breathed on the freezing mark. We never planted beans until after the first of June. One year, however, even in this normally summer month, we had three frosts, and we replanted . . . and replanted . . . and replanted beans.

Actually, Veryl did all the planting and tending of our plot. The children and I had been assigned the weeding chore. (During his first year at this task, Chris – raised in the city like his mother – pulled up all the carrots.)

Our menus always included fresh produce during the growing season. I had only to pick a supply of my choice. I soon realized, though, that this required more than the usual harvesting effort.

I first had to get rid of . . . the snakes.

Eventually, I devised my own successful method for doing this. I just stamped on the ground at the edge of the garden, loudly uttered something like "Okay, snakes. Move!" – and without fail, one or two reptiles in among various leaves obliged and wiggled away. I then went in and picked what I needed.

TALE THREE

Wild Introductions

1
The Birdman of the Valley

AS A BIOLOGIST, Veryl seemed to specialize in everything, a necessary repertoire in a college biology department of three. He taught all subjects at one time or another, from cell biology on up.

However, ornithology – the study of birds – appeared to be one of his favorites. Affectionately known as the "Birdman of the Valley," Veryl taught college and adult education courses on the subject, and authored a monthly column on birds of the San Luis Valley for the daily newspaper.

Local residents knew exactly whom to contact for their questions on hawks, owls, eagles, perching birds, cranes, hummers (humming birds), and any other feathered species. We could expect a call any day, at any time.

"I found this dead bird next to our driveway today," a caller might say. "It's a funny shade of black, and there's some rusty color on its breast. Oh, and its beak is blackish-brownish. I have it in my freezer."

People often put unidentifiable birds in the freezer, it seemed, until Veryl could tell them what kind of bird it was — or until he could look at it and pronounce its proper name. He occasionally obliged these "birders" by driving for miles to satisfy their curiosity about their find.

Our family learned bird identification informally, usually during a drive, although riding with Veryl and his all-consuming interest in feathered species could be unnerving. Conversation could be interrupted at any time with "Look! Look! Look!" – and a finger vigorously shaking and pointing at a sight beyond the car window: a bird perched on a post, or in a tree, or flying through the sky.

Sometimes, though, he deliberately took us to special vantage points.

Halfway down Wolf Creek Pass – a yawning cavern among the mountains of the Continental Divide in the western part of the valley — we'd find a mass of the beautiful blue Steller's Jay at a specific turnoff. In late fall, we'd visit the Monte Vista Wildlife Refuge twenty miles to the west to be amazed by bald eagles populating almost every tree, and by the thousands of Sandhill cranes in the fields.

Soon, through these rides with our own family authority, each of us could identify numerous birds – such as the horned lark, the egret, the red-tailed hawk, the water pipit –most of which I had never seen, or been aware of, before.

2
In His Mountain Habitat

A BIOLOGIST, I also discovered, cannot nurture his interests in front of TV, or even with a good book. He must get *out there!*

So it ensued that almost every weekend we would head for the mountains – never sure what we'd see, but certain that something *biological* would be out there. In Veryl's company, the children and I learned a lot about the ecology and the creatures of the mountains.

As we maneuvered our way on foot around brush and fallen trees, or past mountain wildflowers – Colorado blue columbine, fragrant yellow wallflowers, and many others – Veryl alerted us to wonders on every side.

We discovered footprints of a mountain lion (which we hoped hadn't discovered us), and I exhibited a naive delight when I observed deer, elk, and bear as they walked, stalked, and munched in their natural surroundings. In the less-forested southern part of the valley, near the New Mexico border, we often encountered meandering herds of pronghorn antelope.

But our sojourns weren't limited to animals. Veryl outdid himself in identifying and pointing out differences in the flora. Until I took up with a biologist, I'd had no interest in what I considered "weeds," and "a tree was a tree was a tree." Now, even to this day, I find myself scanning roadsides to see if I can identify the growth there, and I'm challenged to discover the name of a tree if I can't recognize it.

I laughed at, but remember, the name of a dark green ground cover that we came across during our mountain walks.

"That's kinnickinnic," Veryl had said.

"Kick-a-what?"

Veryl smiled, looked at me, nudged my shoulder. "Are you laughing at a scientific name?"

No more comment. Smiles.

For some reason, I found tree names hard to retain — not because they were difficult to pronounce, but because one pine looked like another pine, or one fir like another fir, to me. The exception, perhaps, was the Limber Pine that we found near a forest campground at the northern end of the valley.

"Look at that," Veryl had said, walking over to a broad needle tree and twisting one of its branches. "Shouldn't be here."

Then to demonstrate the unique flexibility of the Limber Pine, he tied a knot in a longer branch, and left it.

I often ponder the reaction of some latter day hiker when he comes upon this looped branch. Does he wonder what freak action of nature caused it? Perhaps a scientific journal has a speculative paragraph about it.

3
Bug-gy Moments

WHEN IT CAME to bugs and insects — entomology, in my husband's domain — my appreciation of the natural world was tested.

One afternoon, during a fall semester, Veryl invited me along on one of his class field trips to a brush-covered acreage, where students were to collect whatever bug or insect they could find. (Laboriously, Veryl had reviewed with me the difference between these two, but the distinction has always escaped me.)

Gamely, I agreed to participate, and I soon found myself on hands and knees, brushing aside weeds and bushes, and *not believing I was really doing this.*

Suddenly, a grasshopper leapt out in front of me. Caught up in the spirit of the class, I grabbed it. As soon as I felt the fluttery movement inside my hand, however, my enthusiasm waned.

I gave the grasshopper to Veryl – and became a spectator until the field trip ended.

TALE FOUR

Out in the Cold

1
Shivering Timbers

WINTER CAME early to the San Luis Valley.

By late September, a dusting of snow on the mountain peaks foreshadowed the deep-freeze ahead. A thin layer of ice formed on our pond in the morning. Coats on our horses and cattle grew thick and woolly. We started feeding corn to the chickens, and began closing the hen house door each night.

When dark clouds released their cargo of snow in earnest on the mountain tops, we knew winter had begun. Snowstorms hit the valley only occasionally, but when they came – the trees, fences, and houses stood starkly alone, awaiting the onslaught.

As though this were not punishment enough, temperatures plunged below zero, seeming to find no bottom. Alamosa always earned its epithet: "The coldest place in the nation." I'll never forget my shock that first winter at Poco Reino. I woke up one morning to a temperature of 48 degrees below zero.

Chris probably railed inwardly at the winter weather more

than the rest of us. Veryl had assigned him the chore of chopping a hole in the ice on the pond each morning before the school bus came (at 7:15 a.m.) to make sure our horses and cattle had water.

Chris never grumbled, though. He worked himself into his heavily lined jumpsuit, donned an insulated face mask and mittens, grabbed an ax, and trudged the equivalent of several city blocks to the pond.

Our dogs and Kim, the cat, may not have been fond of the season either. (It's hard to tell with animals.) Our standard family rule forbade animals in the house, ever.

To cope, Kim spent all night and most of the day stretched out on top of the electric baseboard heaters that formed a perimeter inside our garage.

The three dogs shared one small dog house, outdoors. On cold nights, they crowded in on top of each other, creating the impression that a single large wad of fur had been stuffed inside.

2
Whoops!

CONSIDERING THE sub-zero climate, few ranches provided shelter for their livestock. Our horses and cattle too stood out all night in the fields, somehow fending for themselves. Mother Nature provided their thick coat; we supplied bales of alfalfa each morning.

It would be to my husband's discredit, however, if I said we had *never* provided an animal shelter. Eventually Veryl did decide to build a "windbreak" for the horses near the pasture gate.

He assembled the necessary timber, bought some solid-red

rippled plastic for the roof, and did the construction work himself.

The thought was right; the results were wrong.

The structure's open side faced *northeast*; winter's ferocious winds came mainly from the *northeast*. The only "shelter" our animals had was for their heads – assuming, of course, that they stood "head in."

During the first winter after construction, those northeast winds got under the roof and, ignominiously, blew it off. It broke into a beautiful array of jagged ripply-red pieces as it hit the rails of the corral.

3
Horse Games

I SOMETIMES AGONIZED over those freezing creatures in the pastures; yet they did not freeze.

We certainly found this out one winter night when snow was on the ground, and our family was seated around the table for dinner.

A large picture window fronting our dining area provided a pleasant view of the distant San Juan Mountains during the daylight. Now, in the midst of our meal, I glanced out into the darkness and was startled to see two of our horses looking back through the window at *me*.

Then everyone saw them. Veryl and Chris jumped up and ran for their warmest coats: the temperature was a bitter 15 degrees below.

That the horses were out and looking through our window meant the pasture gate had opened somehow (no time for accusations now), and the horses had to be caught. No doubt the other horses we owned at the time also were loose.

As soon as they spied Veryl and Chris, however, the animals assumed some game was afoot, and took off at a lively trot down the road. The chase went on for a while, but soon two very cold, red-faced "chasers" returned to the house. No horses.

"Well, they'll come back when they're hungry," said Veryl, the philosopher, and he and Chris returned to the dining table.

When morning came, all the horses – with heads hanging low as though sorry for their misadventure – indeed had lined up at the pasture gate for breakfast.

TALE FIVE

The Lady and Cleopatra

A Kingdom for a Horse

HORSES ACTUALLY became a significant preoccupation for us.

Soon after Chris arrived at the ranch, Veryl bought him a horse at the sale barn: a beautiful Palomino – golden tan with a white mane and tail. Chris named her "Lady."

Chris had taken riding lessons before coming to Colorado, and now to have a horse of his very own was to him an incredible event.

He rode Lady as often as he could, learned Western riding, and soon entered various horse shows in the valley and in New Mexico. Too young to drive a car or pickup, he also used Lady as transportation to the nearby homes of friends.

One summer day he rode across Highway 160, just one road south of Poco Reino, to a ranch on the other side. To do so, he had to pass the local KOA Kampground.

On his way back, this young teenager dressed in his usual

jeans, "cowboy" hat, and boots was hailed by one of the campers. Surprised, Chris stopped Lady and found himself surrounded by travelers from somewhere other than the West who ooo-ed and ah-ed at this "real" cowboy, and snapped numerous pictures.

(In some vacationer's picture album, Chris – at the time, probably the greenest "cowboy" in Colorado – no doubt lives as an example of that camper's brush with the "real" West.)

Lady, however, gave Veryl, Chris, and me a scare one afternoon when we were carting her back to the ranch in our pickup truck's stock bed from a horse show in Monte Vista, a town 17 miles west of Alamosa.

On one of the lonelier flat stretches of the highway, the horse suddenly decided she wanted to get out. Clearly she had not been tied down securely, and was able to get her front feet up over the right edge of the stock bed.

Veryl pulled over sharply to the side of the road, and we all jumped out, afraid that the entire truck would tip over.

Just then, a car carrying three local ranchers pulled up behind us.

The men, seeing the danger, quickly ran to our truck; one jumped in with the horse, the others began maneuvering Lady's feet off the edge of the stock bed. The struggle lasted some time, but finally Lady was on all four of her feet and rehitched — this time properly — to her place in the truck.

No charge, they said. Thank you's from us. Just an example of the "code" and neighborliness of the West.

2
Horse Feat

VERYL BOUGHT me a horse, too. She was a Russian-breed pony, larger than a Shetland. Rather a grayish white, a little bit sway-backed, a sagging stomach. I named her "Cleo," short for Cleopatra.

(In the West, Veryl had said, it is the woman's job/privilege to name the ranch animals, and I usually named our horses and pets – Lady being the exception. Initially, I had tried to match our "Little Kingdom" moniker by choosing regal names, but after Cleopatra proved totally "un-regal," I chose future names willy-nilly.)

No one knew how old Cleo was, but I couldn't complain. She was tame and did not buck – a least not while I was on her – and since I had not been a rider previously, fat and gentle Cleo was everything I could have wanted.

(I will ignore the kick she gave me, and the bruise I carried on my thigh for several weeks.)

Veryl, on the other hand, was a seasoned rider. He had been on horses since he was a small boy in the Oklahoma hills, where Indian friends had taught him some trick-riding.

One of the feats Veryl loved to show the family began with his slapping the rump of an unsaddled horse, causing it to rear up, then run. Veryl, ready for this, raced after it. On the run, he reached out and grabbed the horse's hips with both hands and jumped up on its bare back from the rear.

I was always impressed. (Particularly since the last time I saw him do this, Veryl was 49 years old.)

3
Call the Vet

WHILE HORSES are a joy to ride, they also generate hellishly large veterinarian bills. Our horses at one time or another suffered near-fatal fevers, crippling sprains, bloody cuts, and immobilizing bruises.

Our vet (no one ever used the word *veterinarian*) obliged our needs anytime of the day, in any weather.

On a below-zero midwinter evening, while giving our livestock a quick check before settling into our warm home for the night – we found Lancelot (*another of my chosen animal names*) bleeding profusely from the throat. This beautiful roan Appaloosa and our best riding horse had run into a barbed wire fence with force, and he needed immediate help.

A call to the vet.

Within half an hour, a white well-equipped truck crunched over the ice in our drive, and an almost unrecognizable vet – hidden somewhere within a navy blue down jumpsuit, heavy scarf, and face mask – hopped out.

"Big semi's on its side up on the highway," he said, reaching for his equine medicine first aid kit. "What happened here?"

Veryl began walking with him to the pasture to inspect the extent of Lancelot's injuries. "The roan's run into a fence, I think."

Silent, his breath visible in white spurts in the cold air, the

48

vet leaned over the now prone horse and poked and prodded around the bloody slash.

"Doesn't look too good," he said, standing up.

He walked back to the truck for required instruments, then returned to the horse where he worked, barehanded, with skill and determination for almost 45 minutes to stitch up the damage.

We appreciated the vet's labor and self-discipline on this bone-chilling night almost as much as Lancelot probably did . . . until the vet again returned to his truck and took almost another 45 minutes *to write up his bill!*

TALE SIX

Our Creatures, Large and Small

1
Acres of Animals

THE KINDS and number of animals on our ranch changed from time to time. Usually we had ten to twelve cattle, a few horses (although once we had seven), and chickens. Our permanent residents were three Australian Shepherd dogs and Kim, our Siamese cat.

Kim, as our other pets, lived outdoors and loved hunting the ground squirrels that burrowed under the scrubby alfalfa acres surrounding our house. She'd sit above a hole for hours, tense and ready to pounce, waiting for a rodent to make its "last mistake" when coming up for air. Her patience resulted in a fresh kill almost every day.

I could easily have ignored these apparent wild feline talents had Kim not made our rear doormat her chosen dining table. After selectively consuming each catch, she invariably left the less tasty entrails in a neat heap, perfectly aligned with one's first step out the door. We always went through this exit cautiously.

Periodically, different dogs and cats – unwanted by their owners and abandoned in the "country" – showed up at our door or in our garage; or, more likely, we found them eating from our regular pets' feed bowls.

We kept a few of these vagrants — like Skeezix, a black tom cat, who eventually ran off, probably to seek more appropriate companionship; and Happy, a puppy who appeared in our garage on my birthday one year — hence her name, short for "Happy Birthday." But, most we gave away.

One day, though, an exceptional visitor appeared.

I had just closed the gate to the chicken pen after feeding and watering our brood, and, for no particular reason, I then glanced out into the pasture. A large billy goat calmly standing in the middle of it was not what I expected to see.

We were always quite possessive of our pastures because the valley received little rain to encourage grasses to grow. We had even apportioned the number of animals per pasture to avoid overgrazing. Now, here was an intruder, calm as can be, taking his share.

I walked firmly to the pasture gate, opened and closed it, and stalked over to the goat.

Initially, I tried a persuasive tone with this animal: "Get out of here!" – complete with wild gestures. The goat raised its head, but didn't obey.

I perhaps could have gone behind this animal and prodded him from the rear, but instead, at that moment, I grabbed at his large curved-back horns and started to pull. Almost immediately, I realized I wasn't pulling. I was being pushed.

I let go at once and *very* slowly began backing away, keeping a wary eye on the pace of the goat who had decided to follow me.

When I reached the gate, I unlatched it in a hurry . . . and got out! The goat could stay, I decided, until Veryl got home and handled the problem.

Occasionally, we also kept a lamb that we purchased at the livestock auction, although it usually stayed around only a few weeks. Ann loved these animals, and expressed dismay each time we had one butchered to add to the meat supply in our two freezers.

2
Adventure at the Sale Barn

VERYL AND I went to the livestock auction in Alamosa almost every Saturday, an event attended by most of the valley ranchers – each garbed in their standard faded jeans, boots, and a wide-brimmed western hat.

We didn't always buy an animal: it was just good Saturday afternoon entertainment in this small rural town, where nothing else was going on.

The owner of the sale barn, Hank Wieskamp, a short sturdy hulk of a man, both ran the auction and served as one of the auctioneers. He had also been a former horse trader, and now raised on his ranches in Alamosa and in New Mexico, a brilliant line of nationally-acclaimed quarterhorses.

That these businesses consumed most of Hank's time and attention was apparent. He seemed unaware of, or else had no interest in, most celebrities, for instance. And he appeared to care little about sorting out a celebrity from an ordinary customer.

Once Hank brought one of these "customers" into the Lamplighter Motel Café on Main Street for lunch. As they stepped through the door, all conversation in the place ceased. Heads turned, necks strained, eyes bulged.

For Hank, this was just going to be a meal with another potential quarterhorse buyer; everyone else, however, knew he was lunching with actor Robert Redford.

* * *

The sale barn itself was a big square wooden structure painted in "peeling white." In its center sat a large enclosed arena, around which circular rows of benches rose almost three-quarters of the way to a high ceiling. As an added attraction, a multitude of birds – finding entry beneath the eaves – fluttered to and fro overhead.

Behind the barn stood a series of sturdy covered and uncovered wooden pens. On sale day, these contained cattle (mostly Herefords), sheep, hogs, horses, whatever showed up. Each pen had a number assigned to it. This number when called over the loud speaker would prompt a "herder" to lead this particular group of animals into the auction ring.

While Chris was in high school, this "herding" position was his weekend job. His duties also entailed unloading animals to be sold into pens, prior to the sale. Then, after the auction, he helped load livestock into the new owners' conveyances, mostly horse trailers and pickups with stock beds. This was sometimes a mean feat when faced with such animals as disgruntled hogs capable of taking a good bite out of a human, or horses that kick.

(We learned about the true ferocity of farm animals when one of Chris' high school teachers, Mr. Knoop, just 32 years old, was gored and killed by a longhorn steer he had been loading into a truck.)

One Saturday when Chris was new to his "herding" job, he jumped into a pen of particularly unruly hogs to separate them, much to the wide-eyed chagrin of more seasoned helpers. Their yells – "Get out!" "You better hurry on out of there!" – made Chris move fast. A quick leap to the fence saved him. Overall, Chris's injuries on this job were minimal and never serious.

* * *

Inside the arena, an auctioneer started the bid at a predetermined price, keeping up a steady chant that is almost unintelligible until one becomes accustomed to it.

(*I never did.* One week, blindly responding to the auctioneer's singsong delivery – which always sounded like "hang-a-hang-a-hang-a-hang-a" to me – I raised my hand excitedly and found that I had purchased an old cow for $500.)

Two or three helpers in the ring with the animals watched for the often-surreptitious signals from those bidding – a nod, the lifting of a finger, a touch to the hat, a scratch of the nose, the movement of a boot – then signaled these to the auctioneer who, without missing a beat, intoned the new bid, and eventually pronounced the lot sold.

One Saturday as we watched this activity, sixteen squealing weaner pigs ran into the ring. They nosed into every corner, bumped into each other at every turn. *Cute, I thought.*

I was stunned when Veryl, obviously out of his mind, touched his hat . . . and bought them all!

We had no pig pens on the ranch, but this seemingly posed no obstacle to Veryl's determination to raise this sizable brood.

"Remember those doors we bought a couple of weeks ago?" he said. He referred to a farm auction where, in the same spirit displayed when he bought these little piglets, he had nodded his head, and we ended up owning a dozen or so used doors. "Now they'll come in handy."

He somehow felt proud of himself. Proud, I guess, that he had thought so far ahead.

Predictably, after much hammering and pounding by both Veryl and Chris, a motley group of "door pens" appeared in one of our pastures.

3
They Eat Hogs, Don't They?

DURING THE ensuing months, we all learned to care for baby piggies . . . then, middle-size pigs . . . and eventually, sixteen HUGE hogs.

The weight gain of the hogs to around 180 pounds, surprisingly, to me, coincided with the dates of the Tri-County Fair, held 17 miles west in Monte Vista.

One of the fair's big events was the livestock auction, where animals nurtured and trained by 4-H members were sold. (All our children participated in 4-H).

Money earned at this sale – particularly from cattle – could be sizable, and often defrayed a substantial portion of the young person's college tuition. (Seldom, of course, were Mom and Pop reimbursed for such things as feed and veterinarian bills.)

Prior to the auction, however, each member's entry had to be judged, mainly by local experts.

Ribbons for first to sixth place, Reserve Grand Champion, and Grand Champion were awarded in each animal category. Normally, only the entries that earned a ribbon went into the sale. The higher an animal placed, the more valuable it became.

This particular year Chris had raised a handsome black Angus-cross calf (the offspring of my $500 cow, which had been artificially inseminated with quality —meaning *expensive* – semen). It earned the Junior Reserve Grand Champion award, and a good sale price. Of course, Chris was elated. But I noticed his deep blue eyes blinking back a tear or two.

Winning is such a sad-glad event. Young people spend months with their animal, often raising it from birth, and it really becomes a pet. As soon as the auctioneer shouts "sold," however, this "pet" is ripped away, never to be seen again.

Ann and Mark had each entered a hog.

Normally, children work hard and long to teach their show animals commands – a poke with a show stick, perhaps magic whispered words – in order to control the animal in front of the judges and to show it to its best advantage.

Unfortunately, easily-distracted Mark had too often run off to other distractions – like dashing through chico and rabbit brush with the dogs in pursuit of long-eared jack rabbits.

When his turn before the judges finally arrived, his carefree, undisciplined hog ran happily around the show ring, with Mark chasing along behind.

Ann had a different experience.

The previous day Veryl, for some reason, had decided to worm all the hogs, including those for show. If there *are* worms, they usually exit an animal through the normal channels of excretion. When Ann's turn to go before the judges came up, the worms appeared.

So pretty in her new white western outfit, her light brown hair glistening, Ann nudged her worm-excreting animal along nicely, but tears ran down her cheeks and her red face betrayed her humiliation. She didn't quit though; she was a spunky girl.

Neither Ann nor Mark won a ribbon.

We ate the hogs.

4
Intermediate Thoughts

OVER TIME, I noticed Veryl liked having animals of all kinds around, but he seldom showed real affection for any of them.

I once watched him respond to a horse scratching its backside on a new barbed wire fence, which both Veryl and Chris had installed with considerable physical effort.

Veryl's anger flared and, without hesitation, he reached for a railroad tie lying near the fence, raised it (an unbelievable feat), and brought it down on the horse's head as hard as he could. The horse stumbled and fell. It lay silent.

Perhaps more out of curiosity, Veryl walked around through the pasture gate to take a look at the limp form on the ground. After a while, I could see the head move, then raise up. The horse struggled weakly to its knees, then stood. No real damage, fortunately; this time no need to call the vet. But I felt the entire scene was a staggering tragedy.

When Happy, our female Australian Shepherd, suffered a broken leg after one of Ann's friends had accidentally stepped on the dog during a tether ball game, Veryl suggested we take Happy to the back pond and drown her.

A less-than-friendly argument from myself got Happy to the vet instead, and she ran around on three legs (the fourth in a splint) for several weeks until she was mended.

Sometime later, Augie, another of our three dogs, was run over by the school bus that our dogs always chased, as dogs do. Badly injured, he lay in the road whimpering. Our children got out of the bus and ran to him.

Veryl, however, brought out the gun, shot the dog . . . and then we had only two. In shock, the rest of us cried.

In the long run, I suppose I would not have made a good career farmer or rancher; I hated to see an animal suffer or die. I know I could not have killed one, at least not deliberately.

TALE SEVEN

Finding the
Rocky Mountain High

1
Eagle Feathers

ON WEEKENDS, we often climbed into our GMC pickup truck and headed to either the San Juan or Sangre de Cristo Mountains.

The children expressed little enthusiasm for such a jaunt: "Are we going to the mountains *again?*" But I loved the trips.

Of course, I could understand Mark's reluctance. This imp with a chubby face, turned-up nose, and thick copper-colored hair had once had quite a scare.

He and his sister Ann had been riding in the open bed of our truck – probably uncomfortably. (A practice I can criticize in hindsight, but at the time, that's how it was.) My husband, 14-year-old Chris, and I were up front in the cab.

Our truck jounced along slowly, about ten or fifteen miles

and hour, on a rock-strewn road, black lava mesas at each side: a desolate place.

Tracks on the road, however, indicated that a constant, if not frequent, stream of traffic had preceded us – possibly headed toward the Alamosa River to fish, or upstream to the few summer cabins fashioned from old miners' shacks.

We had traveled this approach to the San Juan mountains before – eagles, hawks, and vultures a common sight. When we rounded a bend on this trip, however, we were unprepared for the tableau of two golden eagles nonchalantly posed at the side of the road – their rich brown plumage and golden neck feathers glimmering in the sun.

By this time, Mark had fallen asleep in the truck bed. The rest of us were excited.

Seeing a golden eagle in flight is always a thrill, whether it soars high along the side of a mountain or glides over fields seeking a meal. But this day, close up, the size of these two birds – three feet or more in length – was startling.

As our truck drew close, one eagle promptly took off and soared to a lofty height. The other followed seconds later, lifting into the air right over the rear of our truck.

At that same moment, Mark woke up. His first sight: an enormous bird with its six-foot wingspan spread wide, claws not yet tucked up, beak open – only a foot or two above him.

Was he frightened? You bet! *Hel..l..p!*

2
Head-y Stuff

MY FAVORITE trips were to unplanned destinations. We'd just explore back roads and observe whatever might cross our path.

One autumn we halted for the roundup of cattle by a rancher who wanted his herd at a lower elevation during the winter. We waited patiently, and with wide-eyed interest, as ranch hands on horseback maneuvered an opening for our truck through the hundred or so animals ambling along the road ahead.

Sometimes we stopped to hike — though I soon observed that Veryl walked only in solitude. If he saw one other truck or person, that was one truck or person too many. We had to find a spot that was ours alone.

One Sunday afternoon we headed south to the "Brownie Hills." Veryl decided to stop at a low mesa to check out cactus species in the area.

We all climbed out of the truck, formed a slow-moving, single-file line, and followed our leader up a gentle rise, avoiding age-old lava rocks along the way. Mark brought up the rear.

We hadn't gone very far when we heard Mark scream. The rest of us turned. Oh, poor Mark!

He had stumbled over a rock in the path and had fallen, rear end first, on a large, prickly cactus. He sat very still, still screaming, tears streaming from his eyes. Carefully, Veryl picked him up, and we all hurried back to the truck.

Mark spent the entire return trip home upside down on my

lap, while I tried to remove the cactus needles as delicately as I could. Needless to say, he didn't sit well for some days afterward.

Now and then, excursions just didn't have happy endings. (!)

Once in a while, we needed the bounty of the mountains. Wood for new fence poles, for instance.

For this less than casual junket, we headed for wild uninhabited expanses of forest where our entire family marshaled itself into finding dead aspen trees. These actually were not too hard to locate in a mixed forest of conifers, where the short-lived aspen could not compete.

When found, these trees were dragged back to where Veryl, and sometimes Chris, stood ready with the chainsaw. We could use only the younger and lighter-in-weight trees for fence poles, so lifting and tugging them was a chore all could handle.

However, dead trees actually on the ground were frequently in short supply. Lifeless aspens, though shallow-rooted, can remain upright. Not a problem, Veryl told us, and he went on to demonstrate how easy it was to push these down.

The children entered into this activity with enthusiasm. They rushed joyously from dead tree to dead tree, pushed hard (sometimes it took two of them), then smugly watched the result of their efforts — a "mighty" aspen had hit the dirt.

Chris, capable of felling a larger tree than Ann or Mark, once found a particularly tall specimen on his own. He ecstatically gave it a hefty shove, and down it went . . . unfortunately, right down on Veryl's *head*.

What had begun as gaiety and frolic by the children turned into a flood of words unfit for human ears. Chris apologized, but I don't think Veryl forgave him until the knob on his head disappeared.

3
Snowbound

WHEN WE bought our International Scout – a four-wheel-drive vehicle – Veryl was certain that we could go anywhere in the mountains, at any time of year.

The day before he decided to try out this automobile's invincibility, a winter storm had passed through the high county. Perfect, thought Veryl. He looked forward to the challenge. He now owned a vehicle that, unlike our other cars, would not get stuck in the snow.

Clear skies and sunlight ushered in this attempt on a Saturday afternoon right after lunch. The temperature was quite mild, somewhere in the mid-30 degree range.

As usual for a mountain jaunt, we each carried a heavy jacket but, as we discovered well into this journey, we had somehow overlooked hats and gloves. Oh, well, we'd be back before dark anyhow: we were sure.

Veryl headed the Scout for Rock Creek, a stream on the western side of the valley that flowed down a mountain Veryl called "Old Greenie." A dirt road there climbed high.

When we arrived, we found the way roughly plowed, though still snow-covered. However, our faith in this four-wheel-drive conveyance did not waver. (Veryl's enthusiasm had given us all confidence.) We would give it a real test.

Up, up, we went. Occasionally we slid a little, but no problem. Along the way, we noticed smoke curling from the chimney of one of the few cabins in the woods, more usually inhabited during the summer; we commented on it.

Somewhat farther along, our vehicle skidded into a deep ditch.

Confidently, Veryl got out and tinkered with the wheels to switch into the four-wheel-drive mode; then he tried backing us out of the depression. Rudely, the Scout failed to respond. Another try. No response. We were stuck. All of us, barehanded, got out to push. No response. We *definitely* were stuck.

The sun headed farther west toward sunset.

Then we remembered the cabin with smoke spiraling from its chimney. Veryl felt help might lie there. About this same time, we discovered too that one of the jackets, deep down through a hole in one of its pockets, had a pair of mittens in it. Veryl told Chris to put them on, and the rest of us to stay in the vehicle. The two of them trudged down the road to find the cabin.

Needless to say, Ann, Mark and I huddled together to share any warmth.

A long time passed. The darkness of night arrived; the temperature dropped. I worried about the two fellows on the road, and I tried to bury the feeling that we all might freeze to death.

Then we heard the faint sound of a motor. A truck was coming. It stopped beside our stranded vehicle, and four men got out – Veryl, Chris, and two others. On the back of the truck were a winch and chain. These were hitched to the Scout, and, after some effort, we soon were back on the road.

We carefully drove back down the icy mountain road, the heater blasting warm air into our cold bodies. No one said much. We all knew, however, we'd never again go without mittens, blankets, and food on any trip we took.

Veryl, I noticed, hid his disappointment in this "invincible" vehicle very well.

4
Height Fright

THAT MOUNTAIN experience, as harrowing as it seemed to us, may have been matched the Sunday we decided to try the one-lane road up Mount Blanca, a "fourteener."

"I think," Veryl said, "this one leads to a mountain lake." He pointed to a narrow one-lane, stone-covered road winding its way around and up the mountain like a thin shoestring. (I hated mountain roads like this, and, to this day, I avoid most mountain passes, high or low.)

"What about those drop offs?" I said, looking up at the barren cliff face.

"We'll take it easy," Veryl reassured. "Doesn't seem to be anyone else up there anyhow."

So up we went.

(Always compounding my fear of one-lane mountain roads was a nagging question: what happens if you meet a car coming from the opposite direction? The right-of-way in such a circumstance is part of the Colorado driver's test. I always hoped that both drivers knew the law: *the advantage goes to the vehicle going up.* A car or truck on its way down must stop and back up the road until a "safe" turnout is found: not as frequently available as one would wish. Apparently, the idea is that it's safer to back uphill than down.)

Our truck maneuvered the steep rough roadway, climbing ever higher. I closed my eyes to avoid looking over the precipitous edge so close to my side of the road.

Then, suddenly, the truck tilted.

Veryl pounded the steering wheel with his fist. "I don't believe this. A (censored) flat tire." A second slam to the steering wheel.

He pulled the truck over to the side of the road nearest the mountainside, and there we sat – high above the rest of the world with a flat tire, the front end of the vehicle considerably above the back end.

Perhaps this is only a bad dream, I thought. But it wasn't.

We all piled out of the truck. Ann and Mark ran to find rocks to chock behind the good tires to keep the vehicle from rolling backward. Veryl and Chris found the spare and proceeded, on this dangerous perch, to change the tire. While they worked, the rest of us huddled as close to the mountain side as possible. Of course, I felt sympathy for the tire changers, but at that moment, at that place, I was scared to death.

Eventually, the job accomplished, Veryl got in the truck and headed up the road until he could find a spot to turn around. Noticeably, he did this without any of the children or me accompanying him. We had said we'd wait until he *hopefully safely* returned.

We saw the truck heading back in our direction about fifteen minutes later, and I got in. But not the children. They opted to *walk* down the mountain, no matter how far it was.

And so we proceeded – Ann, Mark, and Chris slowly marching down the steep road, and our truck rattling along even more slowly behind them.

TALE EIGHT

Ruffling Some Feathers

1
The Trouble with Charley

CHARLEY, OUR only bantam rooster, seemed to know he was beautiful – all coppery and cinnamon with a dusting of apricot, green, and a fleck of blue. As I watched him strut around the chicken pen, even I had to admit, "He really is pretty."

On the other hand, whoever had thought up that adage about beauty being only skin deep must have known this chicken. Underneath his attractive exterior, Charley was the meanest bird this side of the mountains.

To call him antisocial would be too kind. He was unfriendly, menacing, man-hating, woman-hating, and, further, he absolutely resented any human intrusion into his domain. Just the sight of a human ankle threw him into an uncontrollable rage. He would scrape the ground with both feet as though he were a bull eyeing a red cape. Then, without warning, he'd fly full force, claws first, into the protruding bone.

Eventually this chicken so intimidated me that before opening the chicken pen gate, I first made sure I knew Charley's exact location. Of course, neither I nor any of the rest of our family *ever* entered the pen without wearing high boots.

Asserting this superiority over humans didn't satisfy Charley, however. He also held a daily competition with the dawn. With some uncanny sixth sense, he knew almost exactly when daylight was about to creep over the mountains, and every morning just before this early glow appeared, Charley's lusty vocal chords blared forth: "Victory . . . a-doodle-do!" And not just one "a-doodle-do." He crowed on and on until every one and every thing was awake.

(I suppose we might have tolerated this particular behavior – we always arose early anyway – had we not already heard from the "Howling Coyotes" who performed nightly around midnight, followed by a rousing chorus from our dogs.)

Why we kept Charley around as long as we did, I don't know. Perhaps we wanted him as a showpiece. Maybe he gave us a chance to gripe about something. Unbeknown either to Charley or us, however, his days were numbered.

On a late summer day just after the start of the college semester, one of Veryl's colleagues confided over a cup of coffee that the small sheep ranch he owned needed something.

"Needs to have a more rural feeling," he said. "I want to hear a rooster crow in the morning."

The patriarch of our long-suffering family couldn't believe his ears. He put his hand on his friend's shoulder, and exclaimed: "I believe I can solve your problem."

Within hours, Charley had a new home.

Strangely, we never heard his new owners complain. Often we wondered – had they had this *fowl* chicken for dinner?

2
Cheaper by the Dozens

WHEN I FIRST arrived at Poco Reino, however, the ranch had no chickens. I had seen chickens previously, of course, but my most intimate brush with them had been in their cooked state – while using a knife and fork.

A chummier acquaintance with this simple bird, for me, all began with an advertisement that appeared in our local daily newspaper, *The Valley Courier*. A chicken farm was going out of business. That meant a farm auction, an activity to which we would later become addicted. Besides the equipment, supplies, and other items usually available at an auction, this sale included fifteen hundred chickens.

We arrived at this event early, and casually spent some time walking up and down the aisles of objects for sale. Within an hour, the auctioneer's chant began.

Once he got to the chickens, we paid closer attention.

The price, quoted per chicken, started at one dollar. Not having much response at that price, the auctioneer lowered the amount to 50 cents. Veryl, a veteran auction attendee, bit his lip. The price changed to 35 cents. Veryl almost gestured, but he held back. Finally at 15 cents each, the price proved irresistible; Veryl let himself go.

We became the proud owners of 60 chickens – all laying hens.

Of course, we now had to get these sixty chickens home. At an auction, I discovered, no one counts out sixty chickens, puts them in a box, and hands them to you. So we had to bargain for cages to put the chickens in, then feeders, then watering troughs, then a stand of nests.

This accomplished, we walked over to the farm building where the hens were still in cages, our choice.

I stared at the hundreds of chickens, listened to their ear-splitting cackles. Then Veryl said, "We can each take two at a time. Just reach in any of the cages."

The follicles of hair on my head froze.

"You mean we're going to carry the chickens . . . in our hands?" The thought of actually touching a chicken, then carrying it by its feet to our truck, made me recoil in horror. *Me? Touch a chicken?*

Veryl raised his eyebrow at me, obviously not understanding.

I smiled weakly. Not wishing to appear unwilling to participate in my new life on the ranch, I took a deep brave breath and carried hen after squawking hen.

But the day wasn't over.

Once we and the sixty chickens arrived at the ranch, Veryl couldn't wait to get some of the birds into our freezer. He found his ax, and ten chickens lost their heads that same day. Ann, Mark, and Chris – each with a pail of hot water in front of them – pulled off feathers.

Since I abhorred the entire process and was decidedly squeamish, Veryl took over and prepared each bird neatly for the freezer.

We lodged the balance of our new brood inside a large fenced dog pen.

Within a few weeks, however, Veryl had built a permanent wooden hen house with a green rippled-plastic roof. He then staked out, next to the vegetable garden, a sizable chicken yard, carefully fencing it so the bottom ends of the fencing curved into the ground to keep out predators.

3
But the Intruders Came . . .

THE NEXT immediate task, Veryl said, would be to train our dogs.

He had learned during his early years on a farm in the Oklahoma Hills that dogs love to eat chickens. Even though he had fenced in our flock securely, he explained, he did not want a dog going after a stray hen that might flap out of the pen, nor did he want our dogs trying to dig in.

As a result, Veryl set up "training" sessions for each of our three Australian Shepherds, individually.

These sessions proceeded as follows:

First, Veryl grabbed the broom.

He then forced one of the dogs into the pen with the chickens. There, he beat the dog with the broom each time the poor beast even eyed a hen, refusing to let the dog out of the pen despite some very mournful yelps.

Only when Veryl was sure one dog got the message did he repeat the process with the next one.

These lessons must have sunk in as, from then on, I never saw one of our dogs show the slightest interest in a chicken.

Of course, we could not train the entire dog kingdom, and one summer after we had been gone an entire day, we arrived back at the ranch and saw white chicken feathers everywhere.

We quickly exited the car and ran to the pen, where three strange dogs were still pursuing our chickens. These "wild" dogs – who had been abandoned by owners and then became "wild" – had been able to dig under the gate and get in. While the children and I yelled and tried to drive the intruders out, Veryl ran into the house for his gun.

Finally, we got the dogs away from the enclosure, and they took off running across the pasture with Veryl in hot pursuit – shooting wildly like a sheriff chasing *banditos*. Unfortunately (my attitude at the time), he missed. The dogs were gone.

Sadly, we returned to the pen and the destruction there. A dozen or more frightened chickens had piled into two corners of the hen house and smothered each other. The remains of several half-eaten chickens were scattered outside. Nothing to do but clean up.

Some days later, Veryl and I on horseback rode along a dirt road a mile or so from our ranch and spied the bodies of these same three dogs in a ditch. Either they had been hit by a vehicle or – someone else was a better shot.

We would always wonder where *our* dogs had been while this invasion was going on.

4
To Make a Better Omelet

OUR INTEREST in chickens increased over time, and our flock grew.

Seed catalogues, which we received regularly, also advertised baby chicks. We ordered some. They arrived live in a wooden box, and we straightaway placed them in a brooder.

There being no place else to put it, this brooder lodged in our compact laundry room sharing space with the washer, dryer, and hot water heater. And on ironing day, I crowded in my ironing board.

Sometimes it was so warm in this room that I thought *I* might sprout a feather. But while I ironed, I found it enjoyable to watch the little chicks grow, sprout *their* feathers, and finally become adult enough to go out into the pen.

We also watched the local newspaper ads under "Livestock for Sale." We purchased a few fancy breeds, then pursued fancy breeds in earnest – a bearded Houdan rooster; Silver-laced Wyandottes; Silver-spangled Hamburgs; Cornish hens; Buff Orpingtons; Buff Cochins (good eating); a Light Brahma; a lot of Buff-and Golden-laced Polish with their delightful crests; Araucanas, who laid turquoise-colored eggs; Charley, the bantam rooster, of course; and two bantam Silkies.

Before long, we had a colorful pen of 65 chickens.

Sixty-five chickens, we discovered, lay a lot of eggs. And we spent considerable time thinking of ingenious ways to use, or get rid of, *eggs*.

We sold dozens, gave some away. I even learned how to freeze eggs – easy after putting them through a strainer. In frantic pursuit of other avenues of disposal, we goaded the children into taking several dozen down to the nearby KOA Kampground to sell to the campers.

But what to do with all the eggs remained a continuing problem.

5

Of Mice and Hens

USUALLY MARK fed and watered the chickens, but I served as his backup. Not that Mark wasn't reliable, or just too often forgot, but generally I found this at the top of *my* morning activities.

After we switched the chickens to corn in the late fall, I found chicken-feeding could also be an adventure.

Our feed corn was kept in a four-foot high barrel in a small room Veryl had built onto the ill-fated horse shelter. (The door was one left over from pig pen construction.)

Because this barrel was out in the pasture, I carried a galvanized pail or two with me, which I used to scoop up the corn and then lug it back to the hen house.

For some unknown reason, no one ever closed the barrel tightly. As a result, "others" had plenty of access. After several bouts with sheer fright, and letting loose hair-raising screams that no one heard – I became immune to lifting the barrel's cover and finding, literally, a hundred field mice helping themselves to breakfast.

To get at the corn beneath this rodent mass, I developed a rhythmical clanging of the pail against the side of the barrel. This, I found, encouraged the mice to dig down, out-of-sight, into the corn supply and allowed me to take the chickens' share.

After I carelessly tossed the cover back on the barrel, I assumed these little rodents continued their breakfast.

As time went on, and I became too well-acquainted with individual chickens (knowing all their assigned names), I found myself less and less able to eat one that we happened to sacrifice for our dinner table.

To this day, I'll select something other than chicken from a menu.

TALE NINE

The Wiggly Ones

1
The Hat Band Adventure

MY BIOLOGIST (and erstwhile herpetologist) husband assured me when I first arrived at the ranch that "there are no rattlers at Poco Reino." He had roamed the entire acreage, he said, looking for telltale signs and proper rattlesnake haunts and hadn't found any.

I noticed quite soon, however, that we had a lot of silver-striped black snakes of all sizes, an occasional large snake that our horses sometimes tossed around the pasture, and a "colorful" snake that my husband couldn't identify because *he* never saw it – *he said*.

Veryl's attitude toward snakes, however, was not just bravado. He held a healthy respect for these reptiles and tried to teach the children and me what he knew. Outings to the mountains always included a lesson on the habits and habitats of these creatures, and what I learned I have never forgotten.

"Remember," he'd said, "you can almost be sure there's a snake under exposed shale."

Then he instructed further: "Whenever we're in rattlesnake country, we're going to talk or sing, and line up single file."

In addition, he made sure each of us had a pole or stick to carry on these occasions. We were supposed to make noise and hit the ground hard as we walked. No doubt the five of us were a sight to behold – all singing a tune like "You Are My Sunshine," good and loud, and poking sticks into the ground ahead of us.

The snakes, however, must have realized we were coming, as they stayed out of our way – *probably watching with tails curled into the shape of a question mark.* Anyway, we never confronted a rattlesnake face-to-face.

Some students on one of Veryl's college field trips into the mountains were not as lucky.

One afternoon, while looking for birds, they encountered instead two six-foot rattlesnakes that had crawled out from under a rock. Most of the class panicked and fled in the direction of the van that had brought them there.

Veryl and one of his students, however, faced up to the challenge and killed the reptiles. The student "snake-slayer," in ecstasy, stuffed the huge rattlesnakes into a plastic garbage bag for future use – as hatbands and belts.

(More than once I reminded Veryl he'd better not bring anything like that to *our* home!)

2
Veryl's Surprise

I RECALL only one incident that strained Veryl's self-assured attitude toward reptiles.

It was one of those rare springs when the Rio Grande River came close to flood stage. All the irrigation ditches in the valley had been opened and ran full of water in an attempt to prevent the overflow. Our ranch too was laced with irrigation ditches, now filled to the brim.

Normally, the amount of water we obtained and the timing of its delivery was decided by the ditch company to which we belonged. Our ranch situated at the end of the ditch seemed to receive water only after every other user had too much – or so it appeared to me.

(Once I attended the ditch company's annual meeting intent on complaining about our lack of water; Veryl had been busy teaching classes that day. I little realized beforehand, however, that when it comes to farm and ranch matters, women may be seen, but not always heard. I also admit to feeling somewhat intimidated that day in the midst of all those brawny "real" farmers and ranchers. I was the only female there. I did, however, manage a question about the amount of water we received. In response, several sympathetic glances were cast in my direction, followed by an abrupt return to "serious" business.)

Now we had too much water, as did everyone else.

If the river could overflow, so could irrigation ditches, and the only way to control excessive water on the fields was through the sheer physical labor involved in closing off the flow into one field, then directing it into another.

Veryl and I did this by hand, every day, until the water level fell.

To open a ditch, we'd dig out and remove a board that sealed off a pipe penetrating the ditch bank. This let the water in.

To stop the flow of water, we'd reverse the process; that is, we put a board over the opening and covered it with dirt.

One morning we went out to the fields early, resigned to another day pursuing this chore. We intended to cut off water splashing into one of our alfalfa fields, then start a flow elsewhere.

When we reached our destination, Veryl, as usual, reached for a board near the open hole, where he intended to seal off the water. Not so usual, however, was his sudden leap backwards, accompanied by a sound I translated as: "Ya ... a ... a!"

Then I saw it. A coiled black snake – head back, ready to strike. (Snakes such as this are not poisonous, but they do bite. They are, after all, *snakes!*) Instead of carrying out its threat, however, the reptile slithered away, and Veryl immediately regained his composure.

He didn't look at me to see if I had noticed his reaction. But I made a mental note.

3
The Windshield Caper

SOMETIME LATER, I discovered Mark was a "chip off the old block."

Finding myself in need of a change from the daily care and

feeding of family and the animals on the ranch – cattle, horses, the occasional sheep, chickens, our three dogs, and Kim, the Siamese cat – I eventually took a job in town with an education cooperative that served the fourteen small school districts in the valley.

The routine for leaving the house in the morning became Veryl first, kids on the school bus, second; then, me. Veryl drove the pickup. I used our blue station wagon, the only one of our vehicles parked in the garage overnight.

One overcast morning, following my usual routine, I entered the half-dark garage, opened the station wagon door, and got in.

Whether I usually first looked at the windshield, I don't know – but on this occasion, I did not. I finally glanced up after fumbling with the key, and what I saw sent a cold shiver through my entire body.

On the glass, at eye level, was the green belly of a *snake*.

Slowly, I opened the door and edged out with caution. I didn't know if the snake was alive or dead. Somehow I made it back into the empty house and, after catching my breath, I phoned the office.

"I can't make it in today," I said. "*There's a snake on my windshield!*"

I don't know how often employers have heard that one, but apparently they believed me because within half an hour two of my male co-workers, Gil and Bob, arrived.

They saw the snake – which hadn't moved – and both men moved in on it warily. Bob grabbed a stick, picked up the snake from the windshield, and tossed it out onto our gravel drive. We all gathered around, leaving a safe distance between the snake and ourselves as Bob gave the rather inert reptile several pokes. There being no active response, we assumed it was dead or close to it, and the three of us left for our office in town.

That night at the dinner table, I mentioned my morning's experience to the assembled family.

Mark giggled.

Slowly I turned my head. "Yes?" I said, eyebrow raised.

Mark's face turned the color of "give away" red.

"Yes?" I repeated.

He lowered his eyes. Then came the admission. He had found the snake on the road while waiting for the school bus, and "I thought it would be a good joke to put it on your windshield, Mom."

I guess I forgave him, but I decided that henceforth I needed to be more wary of Mark's sense of humor.

Over time, my many experiences with snakes eliminated much of my original fear. Yet I cannot deny that each encounter I've had with one lives vividly within my memory.

EPILOGUE

SOMETIMES I AM ASKED, "Well, what did you *do* in Alamosa, Colorado?"

"Oh, I was kept pretty busy," I say. I couldn't begin to relate all my adventures in one conversation.

"But, did you do anything . . . socially?"

Did I do anything, socially? I had to think about that. I was a member of the "faculty wives," a somewhat formal group of women who raised money for various projects. I contributed a few homemade items for their annual auction. One year I knitted a square rust-colored pillow with raised stripes on it; it sold for four dollars – hardly worth the trouble, let alone the time.

Oh . . . and I was in the chorus line of "Annie Get Your Gun," Alamosa's first little theater production. Chris had a part in this musical, too.

As to friends, most of *our* friends were on the college faculty. I don't think I had a close personal friend of my own. Though I suppose, one could say I once befriended an elderly woman who lived alone on an isolated property at the end of a long dirt road – Mrs. Emperius, the widow of a man who had once owned a gold mine. I'd visit her once a week, and wash her dishes, and package up things she wanted to mail to old friends – and generally keep her company. I think she liked that. She gave me her cookie jar, handpainted with red poppies on it, in appreciation. I still display the jar prominently in my kitchen.

But . . . "socially?"

"Some things," I reply. "Not much."

"How could you live through those cold winters in Alamosa?"

"Oh . . . you get used to it." I sometimes sigh, remembering.

"I'll bet you're glad to be away from that small town."

Another thought-provoker. I loved the San Luis Valley, the majestic mountains, the people who knew what friendship is and who care about others as a matter of course. I loved the adventures with animals, the clean air, and the views for miles.

The way of life in Alamosa, I suppose, can be duplicated only in another small rural Western town like it. It will always live in my memory. I miss it.

"Actually, had I been able to," I say, "I would have stayed."

But Veryl and I eventually were divorced – another tale to be told.

And I moved on.

Postscript: Some years later, Veryl was killed in an automobile accident on a long stretch of lonely road in the valley. Ann and Mark stayed in the Alamosa area. Chris lives in Oregon.